LEADERS OF
ANCIENT ROME

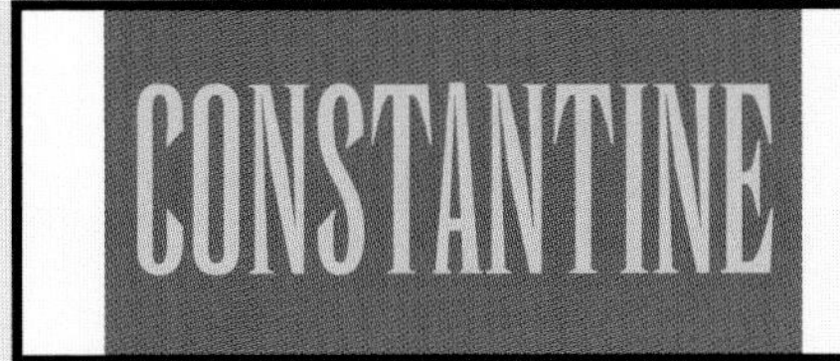

Ruler of Christian Rome

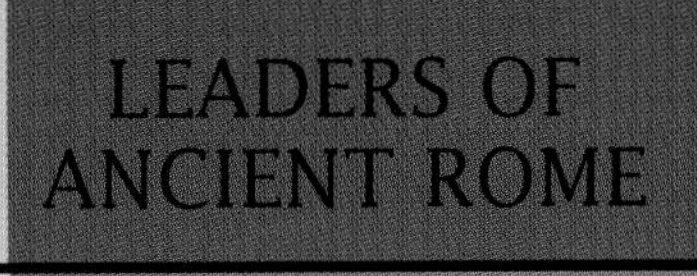

Ruler of Christian Rome

Julian Morgan

Published in 2003 by The Rosen Publishing Group, Inc.
29 East 21st Street, New York, NY 10010

First Edition

Library of Congress Cataloging-in-Publication Data

Morgan, Julian, 1958–
Constantine : ruler of Christian Rome / Julian Morgan.
p. cm. —(Leaders of ancient Rome)
Summary: Describes the life and reign of the fourth-century Roman emperor, known for his struggle to reform the empire and for his promulgation of Christianity.
Includes bibliographical references and index.
ISBN 0-8239-3592-2 (alk. paper)
1. Constantine I, Emperor of Rome, d. 337—Juvenile literature. 2. Roman emperors—Biography—Juvenile literature. 3. Christian saints—Rome—Biography—Juvenile literature. 4. Rome—History—Constantine I, the Great, 306–337—Juvenile literature. 5. Church history—Primitive and early church, ca. 30–600— Juvenile literature. [1. Constantine I, Emperor of Rome, d. 337. 2. Kings, queens, rulers, etc. 3. Saints. 4. Rome—History—Constantine I, the Great, 306–337.]
I. Title. II. Series.
DG315 .M67 2002
937'.08'092—dc21

2001008532

Manufactured in the United States of America

Contents

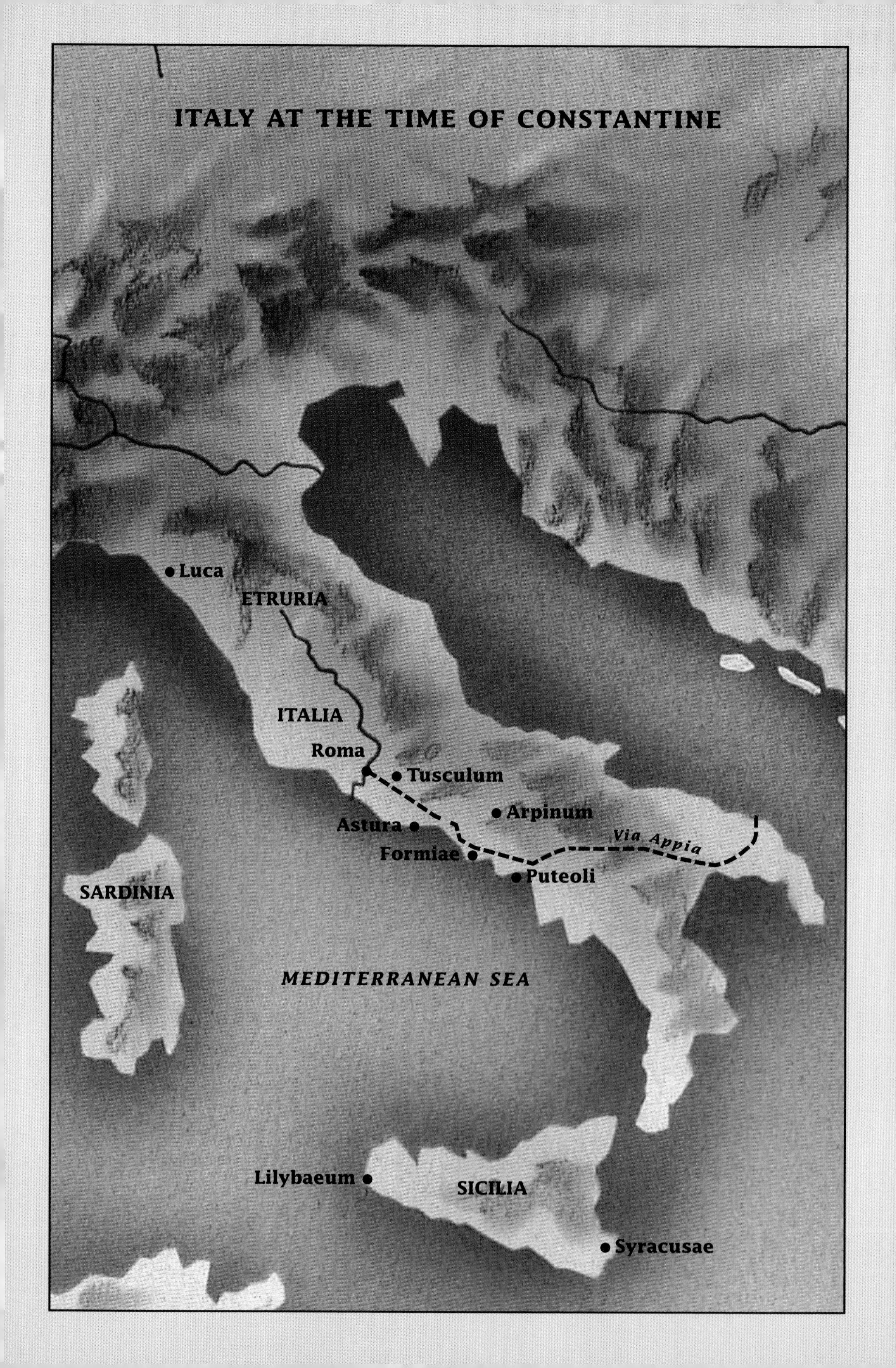
ITALY AT THE TIME OF CONSTANTINE
Luca
ETRURIA
ITALIA
Roma
Tusculum
Arpinum
Astura
Via Appia
Formiae
Puteoli
SARDINIA
MEDITERRANEAN SEA
Lilybaeum
SICILIA
Syracusae

Constantine's Early Life

The emperor Diocletian came to power toward the end of the third century, in AD 284. Shortly afterward, he decided that the time was past when one man alone could rule in the Roman world. He felt that the empire was too big and cumbersome, and that this had caused numerous huge palace revolutions and uprisings. The Roman Empire stretched from Britain in the north to Africa in the south, and from Portugal in the west to Syria in the east.

Diocletian thought that this vast empire could be best administered by a few selected officials responsible directly to him, but having power on an almost equal scale. These new appointees would replace the former provincial governors, whose appointments had left large numbers of men occupying key positions all

The emperor Diocletian came to power in AD 284 and reorganized the vast Roman Empire under the Tetrarchy.

around the empire. These governors had far-reaching powers, but not much supervision from Rome. Diocletian's intent was to secure the empire's long-term stability by reducing their numbers.

THE TETRARCHY

In AD 286, a system called the Tetrarchy, in which four people were to be chosen to share power, was created. First, Diocletian appointed his loyal general Maximian to be Caesar. This term, taken from the name of the great Roman dictator Julius Caesar, took on a new context and came to mean assistant emperor. The senior emperor became known as Augustus, taken from the name of the first emperor of Rome. By the end of the year, however, Maximian had been promoted to the level of Augustus, apparently the same rank as the one Diocletian himself held.

The difference was that Diocletian would remain Augustus Maximus, or Senior Augustus, holding rank above Maximian and able to bring him to heel if needed.

Responsibilities were shared between the two men. Diocletian retained control over the Eastern empire, making his base in Nicomedia (modern-day Izmit in Turkey). Maximian took responsibility for the Western half of the Roman world, running his operations from Mediolanum, or modern-day Milan in northern Italy.

Diocletian's position was designed to deal with potential trouble from the Persian Empire in the east and from the lands near the Danube River in the north. Maximian looked to protect Rome's flanks against the German tribes east of the river Rhine.

Rome itself was not used as an imperial base of operations, a significant indication that Diocletian saw the city as less important than it had previously been. In effect, he saw the heart of Rome's power as being where the emperors were, rather than as just a city in Italy. The mother city of the empire still had an important role to play as a cultural and national center, but its real importance was diminished by this new, evolving system.

The Tetrarchy, depicting the four "emperors" Diocletian, Maximian, Galerius, and Constantius Chlorus, Constantine's father. The sculpture is from Roman-controlled Syria, but is now affixed to a corner of the Basilica of San Marco in Venice, Italy.

After this first division of power, each Augustus was given a Caesar who would serve beneath him, but have almost equal power as an imperial officer.

In AD 293, Constantius Chlorus became the Caesar of the West under Maximian, making his base at Augusta Treverorum (modern-day Trier in Germany), whereas Galerius became Diocletian's Caesar in Sirmium, or modern-day Sremska Mitrovica, near the Danube in Serbia. Both men had been promoted to senior posts from relatively humble beginnings. Constantius Chlorus was the son of a goat herder from the Danube lands, and Galerius also came from peasant stock in this region. The Tetrarchy was now complete with a full set of four rulers, as Diocletian had designed it. The Roman world would never be the same.

Diocletian's reorganizations extended to all of the provinces, where the authority of the empire was made secure in stages. He spent much of his time on the Danube frontier suppressing the Sarmatians, as well as visiting Armenia and Syria, where he reviewed the fortifications along the frontier. He dealt with a revolt in Egypt personally and then reorganized how the province was governed. In the meantime, Maximian was carrying out similar work in Gaul (modern France), in northern Europe. It was clear that the system of the Tetrarchy allowed for a swiftly moving imperial presence across the empire. This had very positive effects in terms of maintaining order and discipline. By AD 298 there was a general state of peace throughout the empire, strengthened by a building program around the frontiers and an increase in the size of the army. Diocletian was keen to promote Roman traditions and, in particular, military discipline, which helped create unity.

YOUNG CONSTANTINE

At this time, Flavius Valerius Constantine, or, more simply, Constantine, was a young man growing up in the eastern part of the empire. He had been born in Naissus, which is modern-day Niš in Serbia. The date of his birth is not clearly known and could have been at any point between AD 272 and 282, though we do know his birthday was on February 27. His father, Constantius Chlorus, the soon-to-be Caesar of the West, was probably not married to his mother Helena, a barmaid. We have very little certain information about how he was brought up, except for some details about how he learned the craft and skills of soldiery in the courts of the emperors Diocletian and Galerius. His origins and childhood were not at all what might be expected of a man who would one day became the emperor of Rome.

A bust of Constantine

After Constantius Chlorus rose to his new position as Caesar of the West, family connections became more important to him. He married Theodora, the daughter of Maximian, in order to secure a connection between himself and his immediate superior. After this, his relationship with Helena was presumably broken off in what was clearly a political rather than a romantic arrangement. Constantius Chlorus urged his son Constantine to marry Fausta, another daughter of Maximian. That move would have made father and son brothers-in-law. Constantine refused, though later he would

At the center of this Roman mosaic is a portrait of Constantia, the sister of Constantine.

indeed marry Fausta. Meanwhile, Galerius, the new Caesar of the East, married Diocletian's daughter. While Diocletian did not want the succession to be determined by family ties as it had been in the empire's earlier history, he did very much want to tie together the new "family" of Augusti and Caesars, and alliances through marriage seemed the best way of doing this.

However, there were other considerations. What if the Western emperors were to get ideas of their own and take matters into their own hands? Diocletian was wary of this, and as an additional measure of security he arranged that Constantine should be retained in his own court in Nicomedia. He would be a kind of hostage who would secure the loyalty of his father, Constantius Chlorus. So Constantine grew up far away from his parents, close to the center of Diocletian's operations in the east.

In AD 296 he accompanied the emperor on a military campaign in Egypt before being transferred to the court of Galerius, Diocletian's Caesar. In AD 297 he again went on a campaign with Galerius, marching eastward against the Persians as far as Ctesiphon, or modern-day Taysafun in Iraq. A great victory was won here, and much land was conquered for the empire.

A Roman coin stamped with the profile of Emperor Constantine

Constantine was a junior officer in the army and was recognized as a promising young man and a successful military tribune. It was the senior Augustus and his Caesar who taught the young Constantine how to become a fine soldier, which was so important to him later in his life.

The Tetrarchy of Diocletian continued to rule successfully as long as its leader remained in power. However, it is clear that Diocletian himself held it all together by the force of his personality and because he always retained seniority over his partners. His original design for the system held that power should be awarded to the most deserving candidate, and not inherited. Also, every twenty years or so the two Augusti would resign in favor of the Caesars, who would take their place. Diocletian decided that he and his co-Augustus, Maximian, should retire from their posts in AD 305 in favor of Galerius, the new Augustus of the East, and Constantius Chlorus, the Augustus of the West. Two new Caesars were chosen. Severus was a friend of Galerius, and Maximin Daia was his nephew. It looked as though Galerius was gaining powerful positions for those who would be loyal to him. Unfortunately for him and for the Tetrarchy, his new regime was destined to come under attack from the outset.

The fact was that two people of undoubted ability had been overlooked in the new power structure. They were Maxentius, son of the now retired Maximian, and Constantine, son of Constantius Chlorus. It is likely that this happened because Galerius's influence with Diocletian was so strong that Diocletian had preferred his candidates to any others. Diocletian had stressed that he did not want power to be inherited, so perhaps it was a deliberate attempt to appear impartial, though that is hard to accept in view of the fact that both new Caesars were so close to Galerius.

It was then that Constantine made a move to separate himself from Galerius. Constantius

Chlorus had repeatedly asked for his son to be sent to assist him in northern Europe, and as he was now about to embark on a trip to Britain to crush a rebellion in the north, he asked Galerius again for his son's release. His colleague agreed, perhaps reluctantly, and Constantine made a mad dash to escape. It is certain that he felt threatened by the combined forces of Galerius and Severus. His journey up through Europe was undertaken with incredible haste as he made use of staging posts to change his horses.

Constantine began to work with his father in Britain and helped to fight against the Picts, the inhabitants of what is now Scotland. After a successful campaign, they returned to Eboracum, modern-day York, where the most northern legionary base of the Roman Empire was established. This was a permanent station where the Roman soldiers kept their camp secure and were protected by the confluence of two rivers.

Constantius Chlorus died here of illness on July 25, AD 306. This was a turning point for Rome, as the soldiers who had served Constantius Chlorus for many years now saw their chance to make history. They proclaimed his son emperor, seeing him as an obvious and trustworthy successor to his father. Their illegal claim was backed by Crocus, the king of a German tribe called the Alamanni, that was serving with them. The principles of Diocletian's Tetrarchy had now broken down, and the system began to disintegrate.

THE FIRST TASTE OF POWER

1
CHAPTER 2
3
4
5

Political power in Rome at this time was largely achieved by the leadership of armies. Each of the front-line contenders for the job of emperor had his own following of soldiers. In effect, the man who led the largest army could claim the highest authority, or so it seemed. The status of would-be emperors was like that of warlords, each vying for his turn at the helm of the empire.

After Constantine's sudden and unexpected promotion, his acceptance by the other emperors could by no means be taken for granted. But his leadership of his father's troops guaranteed that at least his claims would be heard. He wrote to Galerius to explain what had happened in York, and he must have been a little disappointed, though perhaps not surprised, to be told that the senior Augustus could not accept his new status. Instead, Galerius said he would recognize Constantine as Caesar, serving under his own appointee, Severus. This was a good compromise, at least in the short term. Constantine became Caesar and Severus became Augustus, and for a while it seemed that things were working out to everyone's satisfaction.

THE SYSTEM BREAKS DOWN

But this was an illusion, and the main obstacle to the empire's stability came from Rome itself. In October of AD 306, Maximian, who had been compelled by Diocletian to retire, stated his open support for his son Maxentius, who rose up and promoted himself as a new emperor in Rome.

Maximian also stated that he was emperor again, and both he and his son claimed the status of an Augustus rather than Caesar. Their support came from the praetorian guards, the protectors and personal bodyguards of the emperors. They also had considerable popular support in Rome, where the citizens were increasingly concerned about their declining role in the running of the empire. From the

This Roman mosaic depicts the baking of bread in large ovens.

original Tetrarchy, the Roman world had gone to having six emperors, though the authority of two of them was self-assumed. Maximian tried to consolidate the support of the official Caesar, Constantine, by giving his daughter Fausta to him in marriage and by requesting that he should also become an Augustus. However, it was not until almost one year later that Constantine actually used the title. He was treading carefully, carrying out campaigns along the Rhine frontier against the Franks, the Bructeri, and the Alamanni, but otherwise keeping out of the way of the warring factions of his rivals for power.

By the end of AD 307, Maximian and Maxentius had quarreled badly with each other. It appears that each had such high ambitions for power that they could not work together as a team. Maximian sought the protection of Constantine, while Maxentius went it alone.

A gold coin with the portrait of Valerius Licinianus Licinius, who replaced Galerius as ruler of the Eastern empire in AD 308

In response, Galerius sent his co-Augustus, Severus, back to Italy to attack Maxentius on his home turf and remove the usurper from power. Galerius was very upset when Maxentius defeated the attacker and Severus was killed. The following year, in AD 308, Galerius came himself to fight against Maxentius, but he too failed to overcome his enemy in battle. Throughout the wars between Maxentius and the Augusti, Constantine stayed away from the battle zones, preferring perhaps to wait and see who emerged as victor. Maxentius, whose wife was Galerius's daughter, did not pursue his father-in-law, but remained stubbornly in control of Italy.

At the end of AD 308, Galerius called a conference in Carnuntum, which is modern-day Petronell, Austria, on the river Danube. He invited all the emperors to attend, with the exception of Maxentius, whose authority he refused to recognize. His proposal was to recall Diocletian to power so that order could be restored, but this was not accepted. Then Galerius suggested that Maximian should resign again, which he agreed to do. The new Eastern Augustus should be Licinius, a friend of Maximian who had not held the rank of Caesar. Constantine, who had been promoted by Maximian, now reverted to his previous rank of Caesar of the West, with Maximinus Daia as his colleague in the East. One concession was made: They could all call themselves the sons of Augustus *(filii Augusti)*. But this was hardly a solution to the problem of who would really rule. So Galerius incurred Constantine's anger, since for the second time he had been demoted.

Yet soon after the Carnuntum summit, both Constantine and Maximinus Daia adopted the title of Augustus. Once again the Tetrarchy fell apart. Maxentius continued to rule Italy with no support from the other tetrarchs.

By the beginning of AD 310, Maximian rose up again, creating a rebellion among the supporters of Constantine in Arelate, or modern-day Arles in the south of France. He seized control of Massilia, or Marseilles, but was then forced into submission by Constantine, who came rapidly to the scene. Maximian now committed suicide, realizing that his schemes were doomed to failure.

By now Constantine must have regretted very much his earlier support for his father-in-law, Maximian, and he sought from this point on to distance himself from him. He began to claim that the emperor Claudius Gothicus had been one of his ancestors, which was blatantly untrue. Claudius had won a major victory against the Goths in Naissus some forty years earlier in AD 268, but he was certainly not a relative of Constantine. The victory had been at Constantine's birthplace, however, which seemed an adequate pretext for him to make the claim.

After his father's death, Maxentius continued to hold Italy and North Africa, aggravating the problems of the other emperors who sought to remove him from power. His popularity in Rome was still high, as he sought to make his mark by embarking on several large-scale building projects, such as the huge basilica in the Forum and a new Circus on the Appian Way, south of the city. Galerius had more or less retired to his base at Serdica (now Sofia in

A pile of Roman coins from the third century BC

Bulgaria), when a mysterious illness started attacking him, and worms began to consume the inner parts of his body. His previous campaign of persecution against the Christians was abandoned just before his death in AD 311, when he issued an Edict of Tolerance.

After Galerius died, the remaining emperors again began to forge alliances, well aware that Maxentius's right to power would dominate all other issues of the day. Maximinus Daia agreed to support Maxentius, while Constantine

A Roman mosaic depicting gladiators in combat

formed an agreement with Licinius that they would work together to oppose Maxentius and remove him from the scene. It was Constantine who had the most reason to want Maxentius removed, as he had been repeatedly duped by his father Maximian.

So Constantine acted. In a series of swift moves, he invaded Italy, leading an estimated 90,000 foot soldiers and 8,000 cavalry to victory at Turin, where Maxentius's troops had been shut out of the town. After Mediolanum (Milan) surrendered to Constantine, he advanced to Brescia, where he fought again in person at the head of his troops. From there he continued to Verona, where he fought to cross the river Adige in AD 312.

Maxentius's armies, led until his death at Verona by the general Pompeianus, were no match for the highly trained and experienced men of Constantine. Constantine kept his troops under careful control when they were not fighting. He wanted to appear as a liberator and not a conqueror of Italy, so his army was ordered not to engage in any plunder or looting. The final battle of the campaign was right outside Rome itself, at the Milvian Bridge that spanned the river Tiber to the north of the city.

A gladiator fighting a wild beast

Despite the fact that Rome was walled and protected, Maxentius led his forces out beyond these defenses to meet Constantine, perhaps because he distrusted the loyalty of the Romans themselves. This proved to be a costly mistake. He was defeated and drowned in the river.

Constantine had arrived at last in Rome and his victory was absolute. The Senate of Rome voted him Augustus Maximus and master of the West.

STRUGGLE FOR SUPREMACY

In Constantine's eyes, Maxentius had been anti-Christian, as was Licinius, the other remaining Augustus. Constantine himself was a firm Christian, and may have been so for some time before AD 312. Indeed, it has been suggested that his father, Constantius Chlorus, may have been a Christian, too, since he failed to participate fully in the violent anti-Christian persecutions of Diocletian and Galerius, held before the abdication of Diocletian in AD 305.

Diocletian and Galerius had associated themselves with the pagan gods Jupiter and Hercules while trying hard to suppress Christian influence, as this was seen as a threat to the values of Roman religion. We need to bear in mind that the Christian faith held that there was only one god, discounting as false the entire existing framework of the Roman state religion with all its gods. Perhaps the Romans would have accepted Christianity more easily if they had felt that its followers had also accepted them. Nevertheless, Diocletian carried out a program of cruel and vindictive persecution, under which scriptures were burned, churches smashed up, meetings disbanded, and priests arrested.

THE CHRISTIAN ROMAN

Constantine sought to use Christianity as part of his own personal propaganda campaign. He claimed that he had seen a sign from heaven shortly before the battle of the Milvian Bridge. There are different versions of the account, but in one version, Constantine claimed to have seen a cross in the sky bearing the words *hoc signo victor eris*, meaning, "by this sign you will be the victor." From this time, if not before, Constantine was to link his good fortune with his faith and loyalty to the Christian god. The Chi-Rho sign came into use at this time and may have been painted on the shields of Constantine's soldiers. In this sign, the X is

A mosaic showing the pressing of grapes in a cellar

actually the Greek letter Ch, and the P is the letter for R. So the letters combine to say CHR, an acronym for Christ, and the symbol of the combined letters resembles the image of a man on a cross. This is one of the earliest known Christian symbols. Constantine was the first Christian emperor of Rome, and he was about to impose his religion on as many of his subjects as he could.

In the meantime, hostilities were breaking out in the East as Licinius came into conflict with Maximinus Daia. These two Augusti were in conflict over who should control the Eastern empire, and the marriage of Constantine's half sister Constantia to Licinius made Maximinus Daia realize where lay the support of the western Augustus.

In AD 313 a battle took place in Thrace, in northern Greece, in which Maximinus Daia was killed by the forces of Licinius. It appeared that the remaining two Augusti could share power, and that the Roman world had at last found peace.

This was reinforced in AD 313 by the Edict of Milan, in which Constantine and Licinius issued a joint statement to the effect that Christians would no longer be persecuted, and that their interests would be protected across the Roman Empire. The edict ensured that there would be freedom of religious choice for all peoples and revoked all earlier restrictions on Christianity.

The two Augusti shared the consulship of Rome in AD 315. But the truce was an illusion, soon to be shattered by Constantine's deep ambition for more power and his burning drive to be the sole emperor of the Roman world.

Constantine considered Licinius to be in opposition to his new Christian regime. Licinius proceeded to have many of his old political or personal enemies removed in a series of killings. He even had the widows of both Diocletian and Galerius executed.

Christians in his territories were discriminated against in favor of pagans, whereas Constantine attempted to promote and integrate both groups when possible. The Christians were a swiftly growing component of society, still perhaps accounting for only 10 percent or so of the people, but clearly favored by the emperor and his policies.

A plot against Constantine emerged when a man named Senecio was accused of conspiracy. He was supposedly involved with Licinius and the half brothers of Constantine, working to remove the Augustus from power, but the details of the case are hard to establish firmly. However, Constantine had just recently promoted Senecio's brother Bassianus to become a new Caesar, and this rebounded badly against the family. Bassianus was killed, as Constantine showed no Christian mercy at all in taking his revenge.

In AD 316, matters came to a head. Licinius had allowed public demonstrations to take place in his half of the empire against Constantine, and the Bassianus episode had obviously taken its toll. The two men became openly hostile, with battle eventually breaking out again near Sirmium (modern-day Sremska Mitrovica in Serbia). Constantine led an attack by night and, although he was outnumbered by Licinius, his forces prevailed and his enemy fled. In a vain attempt to retain power, Licinius claimed to have deposed Constantine and appointed Gaius Valerius Valens as a new

A mosaic depicting a Roman traveler wearing a heavy cloak

Augustus. Further battles followed in the valley of the river Arda in Thrace. Licinius was defeated again and fled to Byzantium. It was at this point that Constantine and Licinius became reconciled to each other again, with Constantine's position accepted as that of Augustus Maximus. Valens was first deposed and then killed on Licinius's orders. Constantine now had control of the Western empire, including some of Licinius's former territories in Pannonia and Moesia, whereas Licinius held the East.

This division would hold, but not indefinitely. For the time being it was confirmed by the creation of three new emperors. Crispus, Constantine's eldest son by his first marriage to Minervina, was made Caesar. Constantine II, Constantine's son by his second marriage to Fausta, and Licinius Licinianus, Licinius's son by Constantia, half sister of Constantine, were also made Caesars.

Two of the Caesars were infants, and Crispus himself was only about twelve years old, so it can be guessed that their contributions were not intended to be great at this stage. The symbolic union of the families was what counted. Constantine now pursued further military campaigns against the Franks and

A mosaic showing a Roman riverside villa

the Goths along the Rhine and the Danube frontiers. His reorganization of the Rhine frontier between AD 317 and 320 kept him away from Roman politics and civil war for some time.

It was some years later, in AD 323, that Constantine found himself in the Danube area to repel various raids by the Goths, who had been able to cross the river as it froze over in the winter. Their territory of Dacia, lying on the northern side of the Danube, had been brought under Roman rule by the emperor Trajan just after AD 100. Hadrian had partially surrendered it back to its tribespeople, but it had been a hotbed of activity and the Goths themselves had been in rebellion for much of this time. Regular raids into Roman lands had been made for the preceding 200 years or so. These tribes were undoubtedly quite brave and very dangerous, with a fiercely independent nature and a reluctance to submit to Roman rule. But in military organization, tactics, and equipment, they were seldom a match for their opponents. There were now also problems in the nearby Sarmatian territory, where the king Rausimandus was conquered by Constantine's troops.

Constantine practiced his own particular style of diplomacy in the area. He vigorously opposed the raids, but also engaged in a policy of appeasement that allowed many of the tribespeople to enter Roman territory and receive grants of money and land. Constantine's appeasement policy placed a huge burden on the empire, as it was so expensive to implement. In addition, it did not really guarantee the long-term loyalty of those who were brought under Roman rule by this systemized bribery.

CONSTANTINE'S LAST WAR

While engaged in repelling the barbarian raids, Constantine found himself entering territory in the Eastern empire that had been allocated to Licinius—and doing so at the head of an army. This was sure to arouse the old problems between them. The situation was made more unstable by Licinius's increasing resentment of the Christian influence spread by Constantine, especially where it reached lands under his own control. In AD 324 the two men came into conflict with each other. This was Constantine's last war against another Roman statesman, and it resulted in a unification of the Roman world once Licinius was defeated at Hadrianopolis, which is modern-day Edirne in western Turkey.

One leading figure in the final campaign against Licinius was Constantine's first son, Crispus. He was now about nineteen years old and had taken command of the fleet, achieving a notable victory at the Hellespont, the narrow channel that connected the Aegean Sea to Byzantium. This is where Licinius had fled after his defeat at Hadrianopolis. Once again, in an act of desperation, he proclaimed that his general Martinian was the second Augustus, and that Constantine had been deposed. This was more or less exactly what he had done eight years earlier, and it was to have similar consequences.

After the Battle of Chrysopolis, near Byzantium, which would later become Constantinople, Licinius was finally defeated. Constantia, who was Constantine's half sister and also Licinius's wife, mediated between the two men. She persuaded Constantine to allow Licinius to remain under house arrest in Thessalonica in northern Greece. However, within a matter of months, both Licinius and Martinian had been murdered on Constantine's orders.

Constantine went further, having the ex-Caesar Licinius Licinianus assassinated as well. The boy would have been about eight years old. After these killings there was now only one Augustus in the Roman world, which had been reunited for the first time since Diocletian's power-sharing arrangement first came into being in AD 296. Constantine had achieved this by repeated successes on the battlefield. Even today, his ability as a military strategist cannot be questioned.

THE NEW ORDER

1
2
3
CHAPTER 4
5

Constantine stood as the sole master of the Roman world after defeating Licinius in AD 324. It was a world that had been fragmented and torn apart by recurring conflicts and civil war for thirty years. Constantine wanted to reunify the empire and reestablish some kind of order, which would ensure its survival. The system had been threatened not only by the killing of so many soldiers, but also because of the repeated patterns of rebellion and counter-rebellion that had occurred. All around the borders of the empire, other tribes could see exactly how Rome was weakening itself from within and Constantine knew that the empire could survive only if it was unified.

Ironically, Constantine proceeded to dismantle the successful imperial system of Augustus and

The Arch of Constantine, erected in Rome in AD 312

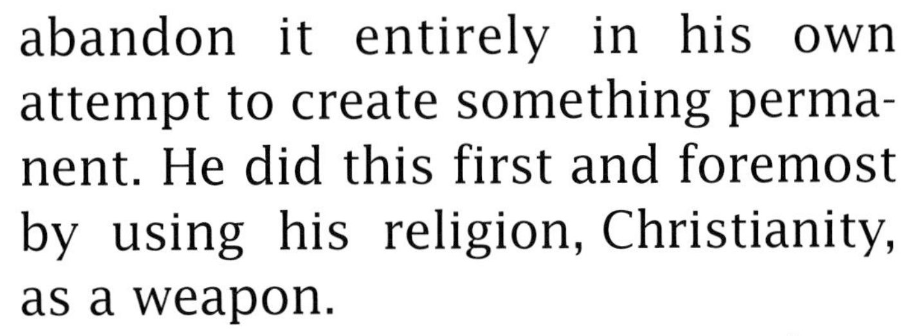

abandon it entirely in his own attempt to create something permanent. He did this first and foremost by using his religion, Christianity, as a weapon.

Christianity meant something very different to Constantine than it means to Christian worshipers today. Jesus Christ was not the focus of his faith and he probably spent only small amounts of time reading the gospels. We have seen how Constantine felt that his victory over Maxentius at the Milvian Bridge in 312 was the consequence of his Christian faith. Constantine saw his god as a provider of victory and success and not as a god who understood mercy or suffering.

In spite of this, the famous Arch of Constantine in Rome, erected in 312, depicts the pagan god Apollo assisting Constantine in his quest. Constantine claimed to have seen a vision of Apollo in his early career. Apollo was associated with the sun in pagan religion.

Constantine also worshiped the god Mithras. Here Mithras is shown sacrificing a bull.

The arch also depicts various symbols of victory. The winged figures later gave rise to depictions of angels. The arch refers to a divine spirit that supposedly guided Constantine, though it is not clear on the inscription whether this is meant to be an exclusively Christian spirit. Constantine had also worshiped the god Mithras, and Sol, the god of the sun. Constantine insisted that Sunday be a day of rest, and the god Sol was very much in his thoughts. At the time, Christ's birthday began to be celebrated on December 25, which was also the birthday of the god Mithras.

Constantine saw no inconsistency in this and worshiped the Christian god along with Sol, Mithras, and Apollo. In his conception, the Christian god could be cruel as well as kind. Most important of all, Constantine felt that the Christian god was the only religious symbol that offered a chance of true unity for the new Roman order he wished to establish.

PROSELYTIZING

Constantine saw it as his duty to convert his subjects whenever possible and he did so in many different ways. He knew that many were pagans, and that if he moved too harshly or quickly in his imposition of Christianity he would lose their support. So he tried to convert them by making the new religion appeal to people in concrete ways. He built hundreds of new churches throughout the empire, and when he came in conflict with barbarians such as the Sarmatians, he offered them money to accept Christianity and Roman rule. Conversion also included admission into his armies, which were increasingly filled with Germanic tribes. Despite this, the Danube area in particular continued to cause trouble, as the Goths and other tribes there could not

A small bronze figure of a household god. Every Roman household maintained a small shrine with such a protective spirit.

be integrated peacefully and reliably into the Roman Empire. In fact, Constantine's appeal to the barbarians may have been counterproductive, as it cost so much gold to implement and also lost the emperor some of the goodwill of his existing subjects, who had to pay for it. Constantine built a new bridge across the river at Oescus in AD 328 to improve access to the territories. He also sent Constantine II to campaign in the area in AD 332. In AD 334 Constantine came again in person and claimed further victories against the Sarmatians, assuming the title Dacicus Maximus, which had been what Trajan had called himself some 200 years earlier. Constantine's achievements had nowhere near the same significance as Trajan's, however, and nowhere near the same financial advantage for the empire.

One of the demands that Christianity made upon its followers that Constantine took most seriously was its demand for moral uprightness. In AD 326 Constantine ordered the arrest and killing of his eldest son, Crispus, in Pola (modern-day Croatia), and then had his own wife, Fausta, strangled in the steam bath at Augusta Treverorum (modern-day Trier in Germany). Shortly afterward he enacted legislation against adultery, which may give us a clue as to why both were killed. Perhaps they had been having an affair, though it has also been thought that Constantine was excessively jealous of Crispus's success. Perhaps suggestions were being made that Constantine had reached his twentieth year of power, the time when under Diocletian's rules he might think of retiring. Perhaps Crispus was even thinking of making a bid for power.

The reason for the murders is unclear, and Constantine often expressed regret for them in later life. What is obvious is that his own authority over others was absolute at this time, and as sole emperor he could do whatever he liked. This may have had a corrupting effect on his personality. He was the man who had forced his father-in-law Maximian to commit suicide in Marseilles in 310 and had had his brother-in-law Licinius killed in early 325. His list of crimes was considerable by now, as he often resorted to murder to solve his problems.

Under the new order of Constantine, his court gradually became more Eastern in style, as he encouraged others to bow to him and recognize him as the all-powerful ruler of their destiny. He cultivated an image of luxury

An early Christian wall painting showing a woman at prayer

and opulence, wearing his hair long and using wigs. He adorned himself with crowns, high-crested helmets, and jewelry. His costumes were elaborate and he surrounded himself with many courtiers. He was keen to have approval and eager to please, but his jealousy and temper were terrible, making it difficult for him to maintain any real friendships. He thought that he was uniquely chosen to see visions and bring Christianity to the world. This produced in him a dangerous conviction that he was always right and that whatever he did would be approved of by his god.

Typical of Constantine's arbitrary behavior was his decision in AD 332 to have the pagan philosopher Sopater killed in Constantinople. Constantine claimed that Sopater's pagan magic had stopped the winds from blowing and prevented grain from being imported to Constantinople. In his zeal, Constantine arranged that when he himself died, he would be buried between monuments to the twelve apostles in the newly built Church of the Holy Apostles at Constantinople, seeing himself as a thirteenth member of this group. Constantine continued to advance the cause of Christianity, despite what we may consider his rather un-Christian behavior.

There had been a perception before his time that Christians were disloyal to Rome, and that their loyalties to each other and to their god were more important to them than matters of state. Constantine did not see this as a threat, but as one of the faith's great strengths.

Christian unity and the support network Christians had developed through burial clubs and retirement funds were forces Constantine wished to exploit across the empire. He was keen to achieve stability, and he wanted Roman interests to be promoted by the Church and state working together. Rome itself was no longer especially important as the center of the empire, but the Church was.

Christian priests in all Roman provinces were encouraged by tax incentives, as church lands were given tax-free status. Constantine's promotion of Christianity was possible because of a general apathy toward Christians in many parts of the empire. The persecutions of Christians, such as those that occurred under Diocletian, failed to catch on in the popular imagination, as religious tolerance asserted itself among the pagans.

Constantine sent his mother, Helena, to the Holy Land at some point after the murders of Crispus and Fausta, perhaps to seek forgiveness for his actions. She acted as an imperial emissary and sought to retrace the steps of Christ to identify both where he had walked in life and where he was crucified. She toured the land, collecting various relics that she brought back to Constantine. These included bits of the cross upon which Christ had been crucified and some of the nails that had held him onto the cross. This was the beginning of a grand tradition of religious relic hunting, which was to affect Europe for many years afterward. Many of its great churches and cathedrals accumulated the remains of saints, old bones, and ancient artifacts from the Holy Land, creating a kind of medieval industry in exchanging and displaying holy tokens of the past.

Constantine kept tight control over the church, appointing all his bishops personally and maintaining a close relationship with them. These bishops had responsibilities for running the churches in their so-called dioceses, or areas of local control. Much of their work was financial or administrative, and there were as many as 1,800 bishops across the empire, with large, landed estates under their control. Church land was exempt from taxation, so there were great advantages if a wealthy man could secure promotion to the position of bishop. Constantine referred to himself as the bishop of bishops, though this could well have been a reference to the fact that *episkopos,* the Greek word for "bishop," can also mean "spy." He certainly wanted his bishops and priests to know that he was watching them and was involved in their activities.

This was because there were threats to Christian unity that had disturbed Constantine's composure for some time. The first sign of a breakup within the church had appeared as early as AD 311, when a group of Christians in North Africa called the Donatists had broken away from the mainstream of the faith. They were named after a bishop of Carthage, and they were hostile to anyone who allowed paganism to enter into Christianity, seeking to protect the purity of the faith after the persecutions of Diocletian and Galerius.

It is hardly surprising that they came into conflict with Constantine himself, as he was much more easygoing and inclined to accept pagan deities along with the Christian god. Constantine confiscated their churches in AD 316, but in 321 he instructed that they should not be persecuted. When the Donatists seized control of a church in 330 in Cirta (modern-day Algeria), he simply ordered that a new church be

A mosaic showing the cockerel and the tortoise, symbolic of the triumph of light over darkness and the factional reconciliation at the Council of Nicaea in AD 325

built and conflict should be avoided.

The Donatist's problem was bad enough, but much worse was the problem of Arianism. This Christian faction was named after Arius, a Libyan who became a priest at Alexandria. His belief was that the nature of God the Father was not the same as that of God the Son. He argued that since God had existed before Christ, he must have caused Christ to come into being, and that therefore his essence was not the same as his son's. Christ was in effect less divine than his father.

This rather complex argument seems almost irrelevant today, but Arianism was to cause huge problems for Constantine in the adoption of the Christian faith across the Roman Empire.

As the argument began to engulf the Christian world, Constantine called the first Council of Nicaea (in present-day Turkey) to debate the issues in AD 325. He summoned 300 or so of his bishops to attend. Constantine grew more and more impatient with Arius and eventually the debate came to hinge around the inclusion of one letter in a Greek word: Should Christ and his Father be called *homoiousios*, that is, of similar substance, or *homoousios*, meaning of one substance?

The council produced an agreement, called the Nicaean Creed, which stipulated exactly what the Christian belief should be, and this interpretation is still used in Christian churches today. The term "homoousios" was kept. The council thus rejected Arius and his beliefs. In English, the creed contains the words "God of God, Light of Light, Very God of Very God, begotten not made, of one substance with the Father." Arguments as to the exact nature of the Son and the Father probably did not interest Constantine very much, but he was desperate to have unity within his church, and this is what he attempted to create in Nicaea.

The Basilica of San Paolo Fuori le Mura (St. Paul Outside the Walls), built on the site of St. Paul's tomb

He felt that brotherly affection and mutual support should be possible for all Christians, with or without the ongoing arguments of Arius, who was ejected from the faith. However, Arius still commanded some support, and in AD 327 he was readmitted to the Second Council of Nicaea. He continued to irritate Constantine until his death in Constantinople in AD 335.

BUILDING CHURCHES

One method by which Constantine promoted the faith was through the building of churches around the empire. His churches were called basilicas, and they were often huge halls with pillars separating the central nave from aisles on either side. At the eastern end there was usually an altar and an apse, a curved niche in the wall. Light streaming through a window in the morning allowed the rising sun to spread its rays on the worshipers.

The city of Rome had a particular significance for Christians, as both Saints Peter and Paul had been killed there. So Constantine saw the opportunity to build churches on sites where the two saints had been buried. The basilica of San Paolo Fuori le Mura (Saint Paul Outside the Walls) was set up on the site of

The northern gate of the walled Roman city of Augusta Treverorum, modern-day Trier in Germany

Saint Paul's tomb on the Via Ostiense, and the Basilica of Saint Peter was created in the Vatican Valley, where the tomb of Saint Peter lay, near the old Circus of Caligula and Nero. This was a difficult site to build on as the land had a considerable slope and the foundation had to be leveled before anything else could be built there. A canopy was erected over the monument of Saint Peter's tomb in the center of the basilica.

In addition, Constantine created the basilicas of Saint Lorenzo, Saint Sebastiano, and Saints Marcellino, and Pietro. He also constructed the "mother and head of all churches," the present-day cathedral of Rome, the church of San Giovanni, or Saint John, in Laterano. This building was dedicated in AD 324, and built on the site of the barracks of Maxentius's soldiers, whom Constantine had overcome in AD 312. Saint John in Lateran was unlike the other churches as it was built inside the walls of the city.

Constantine generally placed his churches outside the city walls. This was not simply an accident. He knew that many of the inhabitants of Rome, especially the older families and the senators, were still pagan in their beliefs, and he did not wish to annoy them by appropriating land in the city for this purpose.

The basilica at Trier

Constantine continued with other ambitious construction projects in the city, and under his rule, the Arch of Janus, the Basilica of Maxentius, the Basilica of Constantine, and a set of baths were built in Rome. Also, the Circus Maximus was refitted.

However, Constantine could not afford to be seen as just a builder of churches. In Augusta Treverorum, modern-day Trier in Germany, a huge hall was built as part of the *Aula Palatina*, or Royal Palace, which, perhaps ironically, became a Christian church in later times and is now one of the most startling Roman buildings in the world.

He also had a major set of baths built in Trier which can still be visited. Other churches were built across the empire, including Santa Sophia, a cathedral at Trier, the Church of the Holy Apostles at Constantinople, and the Church of the Holy Sepulchre at Jerusalem.

The interior of the basilica at Trier

All of the basilicas of Constantine have been rebuilt since their original construction, some of them many times, so it is impossible to know exactly what any of them looked like when they were first built. In particular, Rome's leading architects of the Renaissance and the Baroque periods reworked them so much that they are now unrecognizable from their original plans. However, any visitor to Rome will certainly want to see how Michelangelo, Bernini, and Borromini added their fantastic shapes and forms to Constantine's early Christian churches.

GOVERNMENT

Constantine was not only keen to support the church. He wanted to reform the whole Roman system into a new political order that would relieve the empire of the problems it had experienced for many years. Since the death of Nero in AD 68, it had been clear that no succession to power was assured and that emperors could be created as easily as one could find ambitious men. There had been relatively few times when an emperor's son had inherited the position by dynastic claim. A succession of army generals had risen up at the head of their legions to claim power by civil war and bloodshed. There is no doubt that this had weakened Rome considerably over the years, and that this is why Diocletian had introduced the system of the Tetrarchy to reduce the chance of upstart provincial governors seizing power for themselves.

However, Constantine went one step further. He identified as the source of the problem the fact that the provincial governors were also army chiefs with considerable autonomy, and he decided to change the way the empire was governed and policed in order to reduce the chance of rebellion. In the first place, he separated civilian matters from military ones, creating *duces* (dukes) who would command armies and provincial governors who had no military role at all.

This meant that political power was split between two individuals, both of whom depended on the emperor for their direct support in decision making. It meant that regional imperial power became divided so that the empire itself could be strengthened. Such, in any case, was the theory. In fact, it led to a much more complex, time-consuming system of government, where all major decisions would have to take longer.

The Roman amphitheater at Trier

Constantine also dismantled the praetorian guard, which had existed to protect the emperor and his interests. The guards had served Maxentius, supporting his struggle for power in AD 306, and indeed the praetorians had created many of their own emperors from the time of Claudius in AD 41. Constantine continued to use a body of up to five so-called praetorian prefects, but changed their role to a nonmilitary one. Prefects who had once acted as personal bodyguards for emperors now served in a civilian guise working as important administrators across the empire.

Constantine proceeded to create various new posts, developing a civil service that offered many new career opportunities. He had a series of personal *comites*, or counts, who took on a variety of responsibilities. A count of his private purse handled imperial revenues, while a count of religious donations handled church monies. A new master of the offices *(magister officiorum)* controlled the new, major departments, and was given responsibility for many of the other counts and dukes beneath him.

Constantine kept a close eye on things, however, and a new body of imperial spies was set up to report directly to him. These agents were deployed all across the empire. The counts were supported directly by Constantine, but his loyalties could shift easily in this new climate of distrust and fear, especially if the agents worked to change it.

In addition to the officers mentioned above, tax collectors became increasingly feared in the

The Roman baths at Trier

empire. As the tax burden was increased on the provinces, those from whom the money was collected would adopt all kinds of methods to avoid paying ruinous sums of money to the treasury. Corruption was inevitable, and it entered every level of Constantine's new order. As so many people tried to avoid paying taxes, restrictions on their personal movement and that of their families were employed to increase the agents' control.

Constantine's policy of restriction meant that family jobs were inherited and movement within the empire was forbidden. So if your father was a pork butcher, you would become a pork butcher, and retired army veterans who had sons were obliged to send them to serve in the same legion. Interference and control from Rome was feared, but the empire was so huge that it was almost impossible to exert the same kind of control across all of its provinces. Much of the Roman world began to suffer from a breakdown of law and order. Constantine did his best to stop the corruption and the spread of fear by saying he would deal personally with any citizen found guilty of misconduct. In so large a territory as the Roman Empire, however, that could never have been possible.

The Senate was the ancient body of government in Rome, and it had existed since the city's earliest history some 1,000 years before. Constantine did not want its interference in his new order, but he saw it as a recruiting ground for his growing body of officials and increased the number of senators from around 600 to 2,000. This watered down the Senate's authority, while at the same time enabled Constantine to claim credit for enhancing its size. Again, his policy seems to have been that of divide and rule. From the members of the Senate he recruited a committee that could act with his authority, which helped the prefects to administer the provinces. Constantine spent a large amount of his time away from Rome and had no particular feeling of loyalty to the city, since he himself came from Naissus and had been brought up for most of his youth in the Eastern empire. Under him, the city was in no real sense the political center of the empire, so the downgrading of the Senate was of little real significance. He certainly did not want to spend his time dealing with its disapproval of his policies, his faith, or himself.

A center for the empire's administration was needed, however, and if it was not to be Rome, where should it be? During the Tetrarchy of Diocletian there had been four centers of administration. Maximian operated from Mediolanum (Milan, in northern Italy), Constantius Chlorus from Augusta Treverorum (Trier in Germany), Galerius from Thessalonica (in northern Greece), and Diocletian himself from Nicomedia (Izmit in Turkey). Constantine realized that the Western empire was far more stable than the Eastern empire, and that his attentions should be focused more properly there. He considered his options carefully. He wanted to have a base from where he could quickly reach the lands across the Danube and cope with any insurgency from Persia, where the loyalty of the local inhabitants could never be relied upon and where rebellions had caused so many troubles throughout Rome's history. Serdica (modern Sofia in Bulgaria) seemed an attractive option, as did Nicomedia itself. But Constantine decided to build a new city for himself at the site of his final victory against Licinius. It would be in Byzantium, an ancient Greek city situated on the channel known as the Bosporus, which connected the Black Sea to the rest of the Roman world. Indeed, today this is the place where East meets West, where Europe and Asia are joined. It offered a natural harbor and good transport routes by land and sea. The Via Egnatia was a major Roman road running westward across Thrace, northern Greece, and the Adriatic coast, from which Italy was within easy reach. Grain could be imported to Rome both from the Black Sea area and from Egypt, a major supplier of grain to the Romans.

Constantinople, the so-called city of Constantine, was founded in AD 326. Constantine promoted it as hard as he dared, luring Romans to it with promises of free grain and land. But the established Roman families were reluctant to immigrate to the city as it was very much at the Greek end of the empire. Architects and artists were summoned from every corner of the Roman world. A forum was built and many new churches and public buildings were erected, though pagan temples were forbidden. Books were imported from Rome and other outposts of the empire as libraries were built, while works of art such as statues were brought in from across the Roman world. Constantine saw Constantinople as a second Rome, though the speed of its growth may have disappointed him. Its population in AD 337 has been estimated at only around 50,000, as opposed to the one million inhabitants of Rome itself. Constantinople had its own Senate of 300 members, but it did not have all the officials of Rome, such as tribunes of the people or praetors. Constantinople is certainly the most significant of all of Constantine's building projects. It became the center of the Eastern empire and was not conquered until more than 1,000 years later, in 1453. Now called Istanbul, it is still an important city and continues to enjoy great importance as a meeting place of cultures.

Constantine paid for his considerable building program of churches and the city of Constantinople by increasing taxation, but also by plundering pagan temples and raiding their treasuries. Gold statues were melted down to make coins as paganism began to feel the squeeze. Pagan sacrifice gradually fell out of favor and pagan worship was banned in Constantinople. Despite this, paganism did not entirely die out, and emperor worship itself continued in some parts of the empire. The non-Christian festivals in Rome continued to be held on a regular basis and may have occupied more

Eboracum
BRITANNIA
BELGAE
GERMANICA
LUGDONENSIS
Augusta Treverorum
AQUITANIA
ATLANTIC OCEAN
Mediolanum
Massilia
ITALIA
Roma
CORSICA
TARRACONENSIS
SARDINIA
LUSITANIA
Carthage
AFRICA
Boundaries of the Roman Empire

THE ROMAN EMPIRE AT THE TIME OF CONSTANTINE

than eighty days of the year. We have seen how Constantine gradually supplanted paganism with Christianity and how he realized how important it was not simply to abandon all previous religious practices. The tax advantages of being a Christian must also have helped his cause. Bishops, priests, and church lands enjoyed a tax-free status. However, this policy caused problems since a great number of people were drawn into Christianity for the wrong reasons and revenue was lost as a consequence.

The main financial problems of Constantine's reign were caused by his own policies. He was exceptionally extravagant in promoting Christianity, in his building program, in maintaining a huge standing army, and in using bribery to award Christian status to conquered barbarians. In the time of Trajan, for example, the revenues of Rome from the conquered lands of the Dacians and Sarmatians brought enormous wealth into the empire, enabling the emperor to build a huge new forum with markets that were to be a wonder of the ancient world. Yet when Constantine did the same thing, campaigning across the Danube to bring the same peoples back under Roman control, he not only failed to bring in wealth to Rome, but actually spent huge sums of money in convincing the barbarians to submit.

Even more damaging was the set of reforms Constantine conducted within the empire. By creating so many new spies and officials he was obliged to pay them all and monitor their activities. He also proceeded to divide his armies, creating two types of forces within his sixty-seven legions, which totaled perhaps half a million men. One set of soldiers was allocated to defend the borders, being stationed at the frontier posts of the empire. These soldiers were called *limitanei*, or frontier guards. They were paid less than the second group of soldiers, called *comitatenses*, or escorts. These were positioned some way back from the frontiers, near towns or settlements that they could supposedly protect.

The legions themselves were much smaller than they had been in earlier times. Whereas a legion under Hadrian had around 6,000 men, under Constantine this figure dropped in some cases to as low as 1,000. The military reform was expensive and inefficient, since those soldiers who saw more active service on the frontier were actually disadvantaged in comparison to their colleagues, whose lives were much easier. This led to a feeling of unrest on both sides. Yet again, Constantine may have wanted to discourage any threat from the army, but what he achieved was not what he had planned.

The taxation system that had existed before Constantine had been developed by Diocletian and was based on a fixed annual payment determined by the amount of land owned by citizens. Constantine continued to use this system, but he also introduced a poll tax (a tax on each citizen) as well as an extra tax for the wealthy, senatorial class. Penalties for failure to pay were very high, with a fivefold increase of the amount due for late payment and even a death penalty for evasion. Taxes had to be paid in silver or gold, at least for the manufacturing classes and merchants, though they could also be paid in kind—that is, with goods—by some people. All traders had to pay taxes for themselves, their property, and their employees, which led to untold misery.

Taxes were collected every fourth year, when the most brutal methods of collection were used, including torture. Torture was forbidden by Constantine, but it was widespread across the empire, as was the practice of fathers selling children to pay their way out of tax arrears. Constantine also forbade the practice of tax extortion, where the collectors went too far in doing their jobs, becoming criminals themselves, but this too may have achieved only limited success.

Assessments for taxation were in many cases carried out by town councilors called decurions. These men were put in a difficult position, as their judgments often led to the ruin of their townspeople. They were caught between the rich and the poor and were probably detested by both groups. If they were too zealous in collecting taxes, they might incur the wrath of their citizens. If they were too lax in collecting taxes, they feared the anger of the emperor. Their job was also inherited, so fathers passed it on to sons as the generations passed. There could be no escape.

Taxation under Constantine brought disastrous consequences to the economy, because so few of the farmers and traders could pay. In some regions of the empire that had been very prosperous until this time, such as Campania in southern Italy, the devastation was unbelievable because so many citizens became dispossessed and bankrupt. This was made worse by the fact that so few of the ordinary people could afford to own gold or silver, in which their taxes had to be paid. Instead, they carried out their day-to-day transactions using bronze coins, which became steadily more worthless and which were not exchangeable for the more valuable coinage. This problem was not new to Constantine's reign, as Diocletian had also tried to legislate against this kind of inflation, creating a new gold standard of sixty gold pieces to the pound weight of gold. Constantine, however, devalued the gold currency again, making the new standard seventy-two pieces to the pound.

Constantine tried to fix exchange rates to avoid profiteering and fluctuations in the value of money, creating an economic regime with the same restrictive practices as his military reforms. His gold coins were used to pay state officials, members of the army, and barbarians, but the ordinary Roman citizens were privileged if they ever saw them, which must have caused more ill feeling. Silver was used for soldiers' pay and for state transactions, as the bronze coins continued to lose their value. There is no doubt that Constantine's monetary policy was extremely damaging for the common man, as more and more worthless coinage entered the marketplace.

1 2 3 4

CHAPTER 5

END OF THE EMPIRE

After his final defeat of Licinius in AD 324, Constantine made Constantius II Caesar. This was his second son by Fausta, and he served with Crispus and Constantine II as his colleagues, though he was still only around seven years old. Crispus, as we have seen, was killed two years later, but the adoption of Constantine's sons as Caesars continued in AD 333, when Constans, his youngest son by Fausta, was made Caesar at the age of ten.

In AD 335, Constantine also appointed a fourth Caesar, Delmatius, the son of his half brother. When Constantine died two years after this, power was left to be shared between the four Caesars. Constantine II took the Western empire, with his base at Trier. Constantius II took much of the Eastern empire. Constans took Italy,

A carving from Constantine's Arch depicting the praetorian guard being reviewed by the emperor

Pannonia, and North Africa, and Delmatius took much of Thrace and Greece. Each Caesar was allocated a prefect with administrative responsibilities. It seems most peculiar that Constantine should have done this, since he was the man who had done so much to eradicate Diocletian's Tetrarchy and reestablish the authority of a sole emperor. It is one of the oddities of Constantine's reign that on his death the sole emperorship was again abandoned in favor of a power-sharing arrangement. We cannot fully understand his motives for this, though it has been suggested that he had no confidence in any one individual to replace him.

In AD 334, the province of Armenia was invaded by the Persian ruler Sapor, and this gave Constantine a pretext to wage a new war against Persia. When Constantine died in AD 337, he was about to start a new campaign of conquest in the East, which may

Another carving from Constantine's Arch showing legionaries in battle

have been partly fuelled by his desire to achieve new Christian victories among the barbarians. Constantine had a passionate belief that his pursuit of conquest was divinely inspired, and he may have found Persia an irresistible target for his good works. But this work was left unfinished.

Shortly before his death, Constantine was baptized in a church near Nicomedia. This represented his final acceptance into the Church and was a cleansing experience for him, whereby all his sins would be washed away. It was normal in those days for baptism to be carried out at the end of a person's life rather than at the beginning, as is common now. Constantine had not wanted to be baptized earlier, as he believed that any freshly committed sins would not be wiped out after the ritual. For the ceremony he was naked, and from this time on Constantine wore white clothing and no longer put on his imperial robes. Within a

A mosaic showing the Good Shepherd, a metaphor for Christ

matter of weeks, he died, on May 22, AD 337. His body was taken to Constantinople and laid out in the Church of the Holy Apostles, as had been his wish.

Constantine can be seen in some ways as the last of the Roman emperors, though there were certainly others who succeeded him. However, he was the last to make a major mark on the empire as a whole, and he left a legacy for the entire world by his actions. The separation of the Eastern and Western empires, and in particular the establishment of Constantinople as a base in the East, incorporated a political and religious reality that continued for more than a thousand years after his death. These events confirm his importance unquestionably and may even earn him another title: the first of the Byzantine emperors. His adoption and promotion of Christianity across the Roman Empire had implications for world history that cannot be overstated. The impact of Christianity would reach deep into every area of daily life in Europe, from the significance of Sunday as a day of rest to the development of architectural styles, and even the system of monasticism, where monks would live in communities separated from the lives of ordinary people. This in turn led to the development of

A mosaic of a cupboard containing the four Gospels, from Ravenna, Italy

many places of learning, including universities and schools, as the Catholic Church remained the dominant force in scholarship for more than a thousand years afterward. The organization of the Catholic Church into units such as dioceses run by bishops has lasted right up to modern times. The meetings of the bishops, known as synods, offered a venue for debate and discussion of civil matters, which before this time had been impossible to achieve in a centralized regime such as the Roman Empire.

Constantine was capable of extreme cruelty and barbarism, leading him to even kill several of those close to him. Clearly he enjoyed an absolute authority over his subjects and his family, and this often leads individuals to evil actions. He was superstitious and emotional, and his passionate belief in his god may have tipped the balance of his sanity on occasions. On the other hand, Constantine's acceptance of Christianity did not exclude other religious beliefs, which makes it hard for us to understand quite how his mind worked. Indeed, he seems to have retained some ideas about the gods Sol and Mithras in particular that led him to continue associating Christ with the sun and its worship. Perhaps we need to focus on what he was aiming for rather than what he believed

A Roman mosaic depicting the carrying of manure to the fields

in. His goal was to unite the empire, and Christianity was one of his tools.

Constantine was a manipulator of information and a master of his own propaganda. Today we hear a lot about political spin doctoring, where politicians control what is said about them and how their policies are portrayed to the general public. This was something Constantine took very seriously indeed, so there is really nothing new about it today. He managed to emphasize the speed of his journey from Galerius's court to meet his father Constantius Chlorus in Britain, the swift vigor of his attacks on Maxentius's army in northern Italy, and his right to be sole emperor because of his invented relationship to the former emperor Claudius Gothicus. His representation of Maxentius and Licinius as anti-Christian may be founded in truth, but then again it could

A late Roman baptismal bath, from Tunisia in North Africa

be just another aspect of Constantine's propaganda. The Arch of Constantine in Rome, erected to celebrate his success against Maxentius, uses familiar pagan symbols of Roman victory to celebrate his success, though in other ways he had to be careful about claiming too many victories against fellow Romans in civil wars.

Constantine's struggle to reform the Roman Empire and create a new order resulted in excessive taxation, wide-scale corruption, and a huge increase in administrative systems and bureaucracy. While struggling to strengthen Rome's frontiers, his actions may have had the opposite effect, and undoubtedly he was duped by many barbarians, who simply took his money and scoffed at his weakened regime. More than anything else, perhaps we should see Constantine as a man who never really gave up. While not always successful, he always strove to change things for what he thought was a better way.

THE AFTERMATH

Constantine II became Augustus Maximus on Constantine's death in AD 337. He ruled in the Western empire but was killed in battle by his brother, Constans, in 340 in Aquileia, near Venice, after invading northern Italy.

Constans became emperor of Italy, Africa, and Pannonia after his father's death, and extended his rule throughout the Western empire. When one of his officers, Magnentius, led a revolt in 350, Constans was killed in Autun, in what is now France.

Constantius II was probably the most capable of Constantine's sons, and he outlived all his brothers. After taking control of his father's funeral, he became Augustus of the East. He waged war against Magnentius in 353 and defeated him at Mursa, present-day Osijek in Croatia. He remained sole emperor until his death in 361.

HOW DO WE KNOW?

Primary sources for Constantine are of two types. The written evidence comes from various authors, both Christian and non-Christian. These sources are often biased and unreliable, but include works by the historians Eusebius and Lactantius. Secondly, there is a wealth of archaeological evidence, in particular that to be found in the city of Rome itself, but also in other outposts of the empire including Constantinople (modern-day Istanbul), and Trier in Germany, where Constantine had his base of operations for some years. Many Christian basilicas date from the period of Constantine but very few preserve much of their original state.

Glossary

Augustus The first emperor of Rome, who died in AD 14. From that time on his name was often used to mean "emperor." After Diocletian introduced the Tetrarchy, "Augustus" was used to refer to one of the two senior emperors.

Augustus Maximus The superior of the two senior emperors (plural, Augusti).

basilica A rectangular building ending with a semi-circular projection on one side, used in ancient Rome as a court of justice or a place of public assembly. Early Christian churches copied this style.

Caesar Julius Caesar was a famous dictator of Rome whose name was adopted by Augustus and other emperors to be synonymous with the word "emperor." After Diocletian introduced the Tetrarchy, "Caesar" was used to refer to one of the two junior emperors.

circus A large arena enclosed by rows of seats on three sides.

consul The title given to a very senior Roman magistrate, a man who had reached the top of the *cursus honorum*.

There were always two consuls chosen at any one time, in theory so one could overrule the other. It was originally the equivalent in modern terms of a prime minister or president, though in imperial times a consul was still subject to the emperor. By the time of Constantine, the job had become largely ceremonial.

military tribune A term given to a variety of different officials in Roman society, simply meaning a magistrate, or official. A military tribune was usually a young man of senatorial background, chosen to serve for one year with the army, attached to a legion.

pagan A worshiper of the old Roman gods. The word is used to distinguish Christian from non-Christian Romans. Pagans worshiped gods including Jupiter, Juno, and Minerva.

praetor The title given to a senior Roman magistrate, a man who had almost reached the top of the cursus honorum. It is the equivalent in modern terms of a government minister. A praetor served for one year and then often undertook a propraetorship, such as the governorship of a province, which could last for five more years.

Senate A body of about 600 senior statesmen whose authority combined with the emperor's. It acted as the lawmaking body of Rome, and its importance in Roman history cannot be overestimated.

Tetrarchy A system of rule where command was shared by four people (*tetrarchy* means "rule of four"). It was designed by the emperor Diocletian and first came into full effect after AD 293.

For more information

ORGANIZATIONS

American Classical League
(National Junior Classical League)
Miami University
Oxford, OH 45056
(513) 529-7741
fax: (513) 529-7742
e-mail: info@aclclassics.org

American Philological Association
University of Pennsylvania
292 Logan Hall
249 South 36th Street
Philadelphia, PA 19104-6304
(215) 898-4975
fax: (215) 573-7874
e-mail: apaclassics@sas.upenn.edu

Classical Association of New England
Department of Classical Studies
Wellesley College
106 Central Street
Wellesley, MA 02481
e-mail: rstarr@wellesley.edu

WEB SITES

Due to the changing nature of Internet links, the Rosen Publishing Group, Inc., has developed an online list of Web sites related to the subject of this book. This site is updated regularly. Please use this link to access the list:

http://www.rosenlinks.com/lar/cons/

For Further Reading

Baker, Rosalie F., and Charles F. Baker. *Ancient Romans*. New York: Oxford University Press, 1998.

Connolly, Peter, and Hazel Dodge. *The Ancient City: Life in Classical Athens & Rome*. New York: Oxford University Press, 1998.

Cornell, Tim, and John Matthews. *Atlas of the Roman World*. New York: Facts on File, 1982.

Grant, Michael. *The Emperor Constantine*. London: Phoenix, 1998.

Petren, Birgitta, and Elisabetta Putini. *Why Are You Calling Me a Barbarian?* Los Angeles: Getty Trust Publication, 2000.

Bibliography

PRIMARY SOURCES

Eusebius. *In Praise of Constantine.* Berkeley: University of California Press, 1976.

Eusebius. *Life of Constantine.* Oxford: Clarendon Press, 1999.

SECONDARY SOURCES

Cameron, Averil, and Peter Garnsey. *The Cambridge Ancient History Volume XIII.* Cambridge, England: Cambridge University Press, 1998.

Claridge, Amanda. *Rome: An Oxford Archaeological Guide to Rome.* New York: Oxford University Press, 1998.

Cook, S A., et al. *The Cambridge Ancient History Volume XII.* Cambridge, England: Cambridge University Press, 1999.

Ferguson, John. *The Religions of the Roman Empire.* London: Thames and Hudson, 1970.

Gibbon, Edward. *The Decline and Fall of the Roman Empire.* London: Bison Books, 1985.

Grabsky, Phil. *I, Caesar*. London: BBC Books, 1997.

Many of these titles are available from the Teaching Materials and Resource Center of the American Classical League at Miami University, Oxford, Ohio 45056.

INDEX

L

M

N

P

R

S

T

V

About the Author

Julian Morgan earned his B.A. in Greek studies at Bristol University, England, in 1979. He also earned a master's degree in computers and education at King's College, London, in 1990. He is currently head of classics at Derby Grammar School. Julian has a special interest in software design and has published many programs, including ROMANA and Rome the Eternal City, through his business, J-PROGS. He is a member of the American Classical League's Committee on Educational Computer Applications. He is the computing coordinator for the Joint Association of Classical Teaching (JACT) and has a regular column, "Computanda," in their bulletin. He also runs a training business called Medusa, which specializes in helping teachers of classics use information technology in their instruction.

CREDITS

PHOTO CREDITS

Naples Italy/Dagli Orti; pp. 64–65, 66–67 © AKG London/Hilbich; pp. 70–71 © AKG London/Jost Schilgen; pp. 86–87, 88–89 © The Art Archive; p. 90 © The Art Archive/ Basilica Aquileia Italy/Dagli Orti; pp. 96–97 © The Art Archive/Bardo Museum Tunis/ Dagli Orti.

EDITOR

Jake Goldberg

DESIGN AND LAYOUT

Evelyn Horovicz